VULNERABLE NARCISSIST: 22 SIGNS, 7 TACTICS TO REGAIN CONTROL

TABLE OF CONTENT

COPYRIGHT

DEDICATION

To the survivors...

The instability, manipulation, and impossible demands you faced were real.

They may have shaped your early path, but they don't have to define the rest of your life.

Every step you take toward self-trust, self-worth, and healing is proof that you are building something stronger than what tried to break you.

Progress may be slow, irregular, even invisible at times, but it is still progress.

Keep moving :)

INTRODUCTION

Everything may look fine or even perfect, but deep inside, you doubt yourself, feel empty, or feel guilty for wanting the basics.

For many, this is the silent struggle of living with a vulnerable narcissist. It's an exhausting emotional battle that's hard to recognize and even harder to discuss.

Narcissism exists on a spectrum and manifests in various ways. Most people can spot the grandiose, attention-seeking narcissist, but the vulnerable narcissist is tougher to identify.

The soft, sympathetic facade can easily mask their underlying manipulation and need for control.

So, in this book, we'll help you identify:

- **22 signs of vulnerable narcissists**

- **How these signs impact you and reflect in your behavior**

- **7 strategies to regain control**

But first, let's define what a vulnerable narcissist is and explore why understanding their signs is crucial.

WHAT IS A VULNERABLE NARCISSIST?

A vulnerable narcissist, aka a covert or fragile narcissist, feels superior but lacks the confidence to express it openly. Instead of overt dominance, their entitlement appears through passive, indirect behaviors.

They appear sensitive, shy, and introverted, using passive-aggressive tactics to seek attention and approval. They can also be easily offended and may adopt a victim mentality to gain sympathy and exert control.

WHY SHOULD YOU BE AWARE OF THE SIGNS OF VULNERABLE NARCISSISTS?

Vulnerable narcissists can trap you in various tricky situations where it's hard to see the problem or find a way out.

So, you might find yourself stuck in cycles of self-doubt while they subtly control the dynamic to avoid accountability.

And, in most cases, you'll need to come up with your approaches to save yourself.

Thus, understanding their signs and strategies allows you to:

- Navigate situations flexibly and exit without letting them achieve their goals.

- Manage interactions and set boundaries.

- Turn the tables on them and regain control.

- Recognize the impact on you and find your path to recovery.

- Reduce the risk of long-term psychological damage.

Now, let's delve into the signs!

1. THEY PLAY MULTIPLE ROLES

Narcissists are like chameleons, constantly changing their personas to suit different social situations or relationships.

They switch between roles, like the supportive friend, the confident leader, the jealous partner, or the victim, based on what suits their needs at any given moment.

Sometimes, they'll even mix these roles with you: one minute, they are the helpless victim seeking your comfort, and the next, the arrogant superior dismissing your concerns.

Why

Vulnerable narcissists shift roles to match what people want and create a surface-level impression. This helps them earn trust and open doors to manipulation.

Also, their constant need for approval drives them to find new ways to get compliments and attention. They might switch from warm to distant based on what gets them noticed. The goal is to boost their ego and make themselves feel more important.

Finally, vulnerable narcissists use role-switching to keep their targets disoriented, less confident, confused, and off balance. This lets them destabilize others and maintain control and influence.

How

Before a narcissist even makes a move or starts engaging with you, they'll keep a close eye on how you react to different situations. They want to understand what matters to you and what affects you emotionally.

They may start casual conversations and ask deep questions to learn more, especially if you're wealthy, famous, or just get more attention than they do.

Once they've got the needed information, they smoothly switch up their behavior and style to match what they believe you like. You might notice:

- **Mirror your interests**: Suddenly, they share your hobbies or favorite topics.

- **Adopt your communication style**: They match your tone or pace of speech.

- **Show exaggerated empathy**: They act overly understanding or compassionate.

- **Change their appearance**: They dress or behave in ways you prefer.

- **Match your emotions**: They reflect your mood, whether happy or upset.

- **Give tailored compliments**: They praise your insecurities to make you feel special.

- **Adopt your values**: They express opinions that align with yours.

These changes create the illusion of a deep connection and make you feel understood. In reality, they are designed to influence you and pull you closer.

The effect on you

At first, you'll trust them because they seem genuine and like they understand you. Over time, their constant shifting drains your energy and messes with your head.

You can end up feeling lost, unsafe, and unstable, never sure how to respond or what to expect. You may start doubting your reactions and second-guessing your choices.

When you try to set limits, their role changes make you feel guilty, misunderstood, or like you're overreacting.

This cycle builds stress, anxiety, and emotional exhaustion. And the longer you stay in it, the harder it becomes to trust yourself or protect your well-being.

2. THEY USE LOVE BOMBING

The first move a vulnerable narcissist makes in creating a toxic relationship is to appear excessively loving, kind, charming, generous, polite, and caring.

This is called "love bombing."

It's a calculated tactic to evoke your feelings of safety and affection. They try to pull you in, make you trust them, and create an emotional bond quickly.

Why

Vulnerable narcissists use love bombing to convince you they are the one you have been looking for. As a result, they create dependency right from the start.

That also makes them hard to resist or question.

As you become emotionally invested, their behavior makes red flags seem like isolated incidents. You may rationalize their actions, thinking they are just having a bad day or that things will improve.

This clouds your judgment and makes it harder to see what's happening. Thus, it gives them the power to manipulate events easily.

This perfect image also encourages you to open up and share your vulnerabilities. Once you do, they use those weaknesses against you, keeping control and influence over your emotions.

How

Vulnerable narcissists will shower you with praise, compliments, gifts, and nonstop attention. They'll make you feel like you're their whole world and nothing else matters.

They'll reach out nonstop (texting, calling, messaging) to keep you engaged and always thinking about them. Furthermore, they might even talk about big dreams, like starting a project, moving in together, or getting married early on.

Once they've got you emotionally hooked and invested, they may start to devalue you, creating confusion and instability.

At this point, it's harder to question or leave due to the strong emotional bond they've created.

Just when you're feeling low, they may return to idealization and love bombing, reinforcing your dependency and keeping you hooked on the relationship.

The effect on you

At first, you may ignore or dismiss signs of manipulation and control. Even when you notice toxic traits, you might forgive the narcissist too easily.

You may also begin relying on them for validation and emotional support, giving them more control.

When they pull back or devalue you, it hits hard. This sudden shift can affect you, causing complex emotions. You might find yourself reacting in ways that feed their ego, helping them achieve their goals.

3. THEY GHOST YOU

Once a vulnerable narcissist establishes emotional closeness, they begin introducing instability. And the initial phase involves an unexplained withdrawal of communication. It can manifest as a sudden absence, leaving you trying to explain what happened and why.

If the relationship continues, the behavior escalates into the silent treatment. They remain physically present but emotionally inaccessible, denying responses, warmth, or acknowledgment.

Why

Primarily, narcissists ghost you to provoke a reaction. They disappear to see how much their absence influences you, treating it like an experiment to measure your dependence. If you end up confused, guilty, or desperate for their attention, you're more likely to chase them. And when they come back, your desperate response becomes proof of your devotion, and a boost to their ego.

Sometimes, ghosting is also about regaining control. They use it to punish you for not giving them the admiration they think they deserve. The silent treatment forces you to win back their approval and traps you into giving them what they want.

They may also ghost if their self-image gets threatened. If they don't get the praise they desire, they might disappear and start looking for someone new to boost their ego.

Finally, ghosting helps them avoid confrontation. If you try to address an issue or express your feelings, they may disappear instead of engaging in your conversation. This allows them to avoid accountability and maintain control over the situation, leaving you without a solution.

How

It usually starts with them suddenly ignoring your calls, texts, or messages, and their social media activity stops completely.

If you try to reach out in person, they might avoid you or give vague excuses, making it clear they're not interested in talking.

Sometimes, they act as if everything is fine, and you've done nothing wrong, but their words don't match their actions. For example, you discuss plans or commitments, but then you notice they keep canceling at the last minute.

The effect on you

You're left feeling confused and unsure of what went wrong.

You'll start second-guessing yourself, wondering if you did something wrong or if you somehow pushed them away. Not only that, but you could also step out of your comfort zone, trying to give them more attention or effort than you normally would. You do it hoping to win their approval or keep them from leaving.

As a result, this can hurt your self-esteem and confidence. You might feel unworthy or like you don't matter to them. The sudden cut-off can spark a fear of abandonment or mistrust. And it can make it hard for you to trust others in the future.

If the narcissist does come back, they might use these feelings to their advantage. They may pretend to understand your pain, offering false reassurance or playing the victim to make you feel guilty for doubting them.

And let's not forget the anxiety and stress that come with not having closure. The uncertainty can leave you constantly replaying events and trying to make sense of what went wrong.

4. THEY TARGET YOUR REPUTATION/IMAGE

Vulnerable narcissists are fully aware of how their actions hurt you. Also, they expect a reaction (anger, tears, or complaints) and take pleasure in it.

As a result, this awareness drives them to work extremely hard to maintain their image and hide who they are. At the same time, they attack their victim's reputation or image to redirect focus from their mistakes.

Their goal is to create a cycle where you remain silent, believing no one will support you if you speak out. Meanwhile, they continue exploiting you without facing any consequences.

Why

Vulnerable narcissists target your image to boost their status and gain support from others. Their goal is to weaken your position while elevating their credibility. This helps them maintain control and influence over situations without confrontation.

If you try to call them out or defend yourself, you might be in for a surprise. People can end up believing their version of events, even if it's twisted.

They may also use this tactic to isolate you. They manipulate others and turn them against you to damage your relationships. This isolation makes you more vulnerable to further manipulation and allows their harmful behavior to continue without consequences.

How

Vulnerable narcissists might exaggerate your mistakes or weaknesses to make you look incompetent or unreliable.

You might notice that when you're around other people, they suddenly start criticizing you or trying to make you look bad.

They could also spread false information or twist the facts to damage your reputation.

They might even attack your relationships, making you look bad just for being connected with certain people. For example, they might attack your friends in public and then criticize you for being friends with them.

Finally, they talk about you when you're not around. They plant seeds of doubt about your character, intentions, or reliability, so that by the time you try to defend yourself, their version of the story has already taken hold.

The effect on you

A bad reputation can harm your relationships. When others believe the narcissist's lies, your belonging disappears, your community slips away, and you're left isolated without support.

This negative perception can also close many doors, whether in your career, social life, or personal connections. Others may hesitate to hire, trust, or work with you, retarding your growth and progress.

Also, being constantly judged or labeled negatively can hurt your self-esteem. You might begin to believe what others say about you. This can make you feel ashamed or like you're not good enough.

Finally, you might find yourself stuck in a never-ending cycle of trying to clear your name. This constant inner struggle can lead to frustration, anger, or even depression as you attempt to change how people view you.

5. THEY PROJECT

Self-projection is an unconscious process where the vulnerable narcissist attributes their insecurities, fears, or negative traits to you. If they feel envy towards a friend's success, they will project that envy and accuse the friend of being jealous of them.

Why

A vulnerable narcissist projects onto their victim mainly as a defense mechanism to feel safe. They shield themselves from facing their flaws or the shame associated with their actions.

Beyond self-protection, vulnerable narcissists expect others to judge them, criticize them, or uncover "the truth" about them, which they perceive as threatening. Projection allows them to invert reality. They become the blameless party, while you are cast as the villain.

Finally, if they can make you appear at fault, they avoid admitting responsibility altogether. And you end up taking responsibility for their actions.

How

Vulnerable narcissists use a range of techniques to project their self-worth onto you.

They launch direct accusations, blaming you for the very things they are guilty of. They also assume your intentions, claiming they know what you're "really" thinking, and always cast it negatively.

Furthermore, they provoke emotional reactions, then point to your anger as "proof" that you're the bad one. Not only that, but they nitpick minor flaws to magnify them, making themselves appear superior.

Finally, they shift blame and gaslight you, insisting your past actions forced them to behave badly.

The effect on you

At first, projection triggers confusion and self-doubt. You find yourself becoming defensive and over-explaining, trying to prove you're not what they accuse you of.

Also, their constant nitpicking, blame-shifting, and negative assumptions wear you down. You begin to internalize their criticism, and your confidence in your judgment declines.

Soon, you become hypervigilant, overly alert to their moods and behaviors, always trying to anticipate the next attack.

In the end, you are left carrying all the "badness" they refused to own, while they walk away feeling like the blameless party.

6. THEY WEAPONIZE ASSISTANCE

Vulnerable narcissists offer help, advice, or support in a way that appears helpful but is harmful. The "assistance" is done poorly, incompletely, or on their terms.

You might ask them to do something simple, like clean or organize, but they'll do it in a way that doesn't meet your expectations.

They might put things in the wrong place, skip steps, or do it halfheartedly. Then, because the task isn't done "correctly," you end up redoing it yourself.

Why

Vulnerable narcissists weaponize helpful acts to express resentment, assert dominance, remind you of their superiority, create obligation, provoke tension, and punish or manipulate you.

It's a subtle form of retaliation or passive aggression that provides a covert channel for hostility without confrontation. This allows them to maintain the appearance of being a "good" or "generous" person.

Furthermore, provoking confusion, guilt, or anger through "help" gives them leverage. Your reactions become a tool for them to justify their narrative that you're the problem, the unstable one, the ungrateful one, the one who can't be satisfied.

How

They may first insert themselves into your situation, offering solutions to problems that didn't exist, or ones they may have subtly created.

And even when there's a clear or reasonable way to do something, they insist on doing it their way, which introduces tension from the start.

If you ask for something specific, they agree, but complete it incorrectly, partially, or in a way that creates more work for you. For example, you ask them to clean, and they leave things out of place, so you have to redo it.

When you point out the issue, the focus shifts. Instead of addressing the poor execution, they paint you as ungrateful: "I tried to help, and you're still not satisfied." The original request gets buried under guilt, and your reasonable correction is seen as criticism.

The effect on you

First, the burnout. Constantly monitoring, redoing, or emotionally managing someone else's "help" is exhausting. It drains the motivation that drives you to take on a role and leaves you disconnected from people and your environment. You start feeling ineffective or thinking that nothing you do matters.

This constant strain conditions your brain to associate help or any activity with stress, guilt, and extra labor. As a result, you stop delegating, procrastinate, or even avoid starting tasks altogether. What looks like laziness is your mind trying to preserve energy and reduce friction.

Finally, you stop asking for help entirely. You also suppress valid feedback, disengage from friends, family, and colleagues, and struggle to gain the energy to start or finish tasks.

7. THEY COMMAND INSTEAD OF COLLABORATING

Imagine this: You're enjoying a quiet moment, maybe reading a book or sipping a cup of tea.

Suddenly, the narcissist comes up and says, "You will come with me to pick up some things." There is no request, no preamble, no consideration for your time. They simply expect you to drop everything and comply whenever it suits them, regardless of your plans or feelings.

That's how narcissists function. They put their needs and desires at the forefront, completely ignoring your boundaries and responsibilities. Their entitlement leads them to believe that your time and energy are theirs to control.

Why

Vulnerable narcissists build exploitative relationships.

To them, people aren't equals. They're resources to be used when required. This mindset allows them to disregard the feelings or needs of those around them. When they make requests, it's always about what they want. There's little to no consideration for how their demands may affect others.

They also have a strong sense of entitlement, assuming that they deserve special treatment or recognition simply because they exist. They don't see the need to acknowledge or meet the needs of others because they view themselves as more important. And this mindset leads them to expect others to cater to their desires without offering anything in return.

Finally, collaboration relies on transparency, honesty, and mutual respect. These qualities require vulnerable narcissists to share control and power. This signals potential loss of control, so they resist asking for permission, avoid delegating authority, and situations where others might have influence.

How

Vulnerable narcissists command in subtle yet manipulative ways.

At first, they might come across as polite or even a bit caring, asking for your help with something. But that friendly façade can change quickly.

For example, they might start with, "Could you help me with this?" But before long, it turns into, "You need to do this for me."

Then, they might do something minimal for you, like a small favor or just showing a little interest, and suddenly, they feel entitled to dictate your actions. They'll make you feel like you owe them, creating a sense of obligation.

And if you hesitate or say no? That's when the emotional pressure ramps up. They might react with anger, guilt-trip you, or even play the victim, making their request seem urgent or essential.

The effect on you

When narcissists demand immediate compliance, they disrupt your routine and ignore your commitments. This creates a constant sense of urgency, where your time and priorities take a backseat to theirs.

You find yourself adjusting plans, canceling important tasks, or rushing to meet their demands. The struggle drains your emotions, leaving little energy for your life.

Their behavior also teaches you to hurry through everyday moments (speaking faster, walking quicker) as if someone is about to steal your time.

Furthermore, narcissists make it hard to say "No." When you do, they push back, guilt-trip you, or manipulate you into feeling bad. This cultivates a sense of obligation and strengthens their control over you.

You may also find yourself putting others' needs first for no clear reason, almost automatically. This comes from the pressure of the obligation they instill in you.

When you try to prioritize your needs, you may feel guilty for standing up for yourself, making you more vulnerable to their manipulation. Each time you give in, slide further from your boundaries and into their control.

8. THEY MANIPULATE YOUR EMOTIONS

Narcissists try to control how you feel to maintain power and meet their needs.

They manipulate your emotional reactions to influence your behavior and decision-making. For instance, they might provoke conflicts to divert your attention from their actions or to make you more submissive.

Why

Narcissists rely on emotional manipulation to maintain control and boost their superiority. This technique allows them to stay dominant, steering decisions and interactions to benefit their interests.

Additionally, their manipulation keeps you distracted, unsure, and insecure about your feelings and perceptions.

As a result, you're less likely to challenge their behavior or prioritize your needs. This makes it easier for them to keep controlling you.

The more they play with your emotions, the more you second-guess yourself, making you more likely to give in to their demands, even if it hurts you in the process.

How

To begin with, narcissists use guilt to make you believe you're the cause of their emotional concerns.

For instance, they might hint that their unhappiness is because of something you did, or didn't do. And the goal is to make you feel responsible for their feelings, pushing you to always be there for them and cater to their needs.

Furthermore, they might blow up over small issues, creating chaos and uncertainty. This leaves you walking on eggshells, constantly trying to manage their emotions and avoid triggering an outburst.

In addition, vulnerable narcissists frequently play the victim to gain sympathy and attention. As a result, you may find yourself more focused on seeking their approval and meeting their demands.

They might also play games with approval and affection, giving it when it's convenient, and taking it away when they get what they want. This keeps you on edge, always trying to stay in their good graces.

Finally, instead of being direct about their needs or frustrations, they might use passive-aggressive tactics like giving you silent treatment or making snide remarks. This leaves you confused and anxious, making you more vulnerable to their emotional manipulation.

The effect on you

You might find it hard to make clear decisions or keep your emotions steady. For instance, setting and maintaining healthy boundaries becomes tricky because manipulative behavior blurs what's acceptable and what's not.

It can even lead to mental health problems. You might feel persistently sad, hopeless, or unmotivated.

In some cases, the ongoing stress and emotional strain can even contribute to conditions like Attention Deficit Hyperactivity Disorder (ADHD).

Furthermore, dealing with the manipulator's behavior might affect how you interact with friends and family, making communication and connections more difficult.

9. THEY GASLIGHT YOU

Gaslighting is a sneaky form of manipulation, where a vulnerable narcissist slowly messes with your judgments.

Instead of just outright lying or denying things, they use more indirect tactics to make you question your thoughts and perceptions. You might not even realize it's happening until it's too late, which strengthens the narcissist's hold over you.

Their goal is to shake your confidence, make you doubt yourself, and keep you under their influence without consequences.

Why

Vulnerable narcissists use gaslighting to protect themselves and control their narrative. This calculated manipulation leaves you uncertain, confused, and reliant on their version of the truth.

By doing this, they appear more reasonable and enhance their credibility. It also allows them to gain validation and support from others.

Additionally, gaslighting helps them shift the blame onto you, making you feel guilty and framing themselves as the victim or the rational one. This enables them to evade responsibility for their actions.

How

Vulnerable narcissists use various tactics to distort reality and undermine your confidence.

First, they minimize their hurtful behavior, making you feel like you are overreacting or imagining things. For instance, if they have been dismissive, they might say, "You're just being too sensitive," even if their behavior was hurtful.

They also act like they're unaware of how their actions or comments affect you, even though they're fully aware of what they're doing. A common phrase might be, *I didn't mean to upset you,* when their actions were deliberately harmful.

When you confront them about their actions, they shift the blame onto you, saying things like, *If you hadn't done that, I wouldn't have reacted this way,* to justify their inappropriate behavior.

Furthermore, they subtly undermine your confidence by questioning your memory or understanding of events. They might say things like, "I don't remember it that way," or "Are you sure that's what happened?" This can cause you to doubt your memories.

Finally, they mix truth with lies or give you conflicting stories, making it hard to know what's real. That keeps you second-guessing yourself and struggling to figure out what's going on.

The effect on you

Subtle gaslighting can harm your confidence in your perceptions, memories, and judgment. Repeated manipulation can lead you to doubt your abilities and decisions.

As your self-trust diminishes, you may begin relying more on the narcissist for validation and guidance, unintentionally giving them greater control over your thoughts and actions.

This growing dependence deepens their influence, leaving you isolated and trapped.

Eventually, breaking free from their toxic grip becomes incredibly challenging, as your sense of self becomes intertwined with their approval.

10. THEY INDULGE IN SELF-PITY

Vulnerable narcissists are experts at acting hurt and feeling sorry for themselves. They know how to manipulate situations to draw sympathy and attention.

They exaggerate their struggles, acting like they're always at the mercy of their circumstances. It's like they want to be seen as the victim in every scenario.

Sometimes, it's their way of making everything about them, positioning themselves as the main character in any scenario. They twist events to fit their narrative of being the innocent, wronged party.

Why

Vulnerable narcissists portray themselves as constantly suffering or misunderstood to manipulate others. By gaining sympathy, they secure additional care, support, or special treatment.

They also use self-pity to excuse their actions, blaming their behavior on their supposed pain.

At the same time, their focus on their suffering allows them to easily ignore the needs and feelings of others, avoiding any responsibility to help.

How

Vulnerable narcissists exaggerate their problems, making them seem worse than they are.

They might say, *"I always get the short end of the stick,"* to gain sympathy. They focus on how unfairly they've been treated and shift blame to others. For example, *"I'm always passed over for promotions. No one appreciates my hard work. It's so unfair."*

They also highlight their sacrifices to seek validation, claiming no one notices their efforts. *"I always put everyone else's needs first, but no one sees how much I do. It's like I'm invisible."*

Finally, instead of taking responsibility for issues, they blame others. *"I wouldn't be in this mess if it weren't for how selfish my friends are. They never think about how their actions affect me."*

The effect on you

Before you know it, you may find yourself giving them more care and attention than they deserve, strengthening their control over you.

In the process, you might neglect your needs and feelings while trying to support the narcissist, causing emotional stress.

As they keep playing the victim, and you try to make things easier for them, guilt can start to creep in. You may begin questioning if you're being too harsh or unreasonable.

Their behavior can leave you doubting whether you're being fair or if they're truly as mistreated as they claim.

11. THEY USE PASSIVE-AGGRESSIVE

Vulnerable narcissists use indirect aggression. They express hostility through passive-aggressive behavior rather than confrontation.

They belittle or undermine you while pretending to be kind or innocent. This makes it hard to see their true intentions and hold them accountable.

Why

The first reason is that they are weak and lack emotional resilience.

They use subtle aggression to appear innocent, allowing them to manipulate situations, stay in control, and avoid direct criticism. It makes it difficult for you to call them out on their behavior.

This tactic also helps them protect their carefully crafted image, whether as the supporter or the victim. Since their aggression is subtle, they can easily deny any wrongdoing and maintain the facade of being misunderstood or mistreated.

Furthermore, by keeping things indirect, they obscure the real issues and make it hard to tackle the fundamental disagreements. This way, they avoid facing immediate consequences or accountability.

How

Vulnerable narcissists disguise their hostility with backhanded compliments or veiled insults.

They pretend to be supportive while undermining you. For example, they might say, *"You're so brave for wearing that outfit. Not everyone could pull it off."* This sounds like praise, but it questions your choices.

They may also invalidate your efforts or achievements in subtle ways. They could spread rumors, diminish your accomplishments, or set up obstacles to sabotage your success or reputation.

In addition, they drop passive-aggressive comments or jokes that reveal their true feelings. For instance, they might say, *"Must be nice to have so much free time. I can't imagine what that's like."* This hints at jealousy while pretending to be light-hearted.

The effect on you

Since subtle aggression isn't direct, it's difficult to confront or address.

You might struggle to pinpoint the real issues because they are hidden behind passive-aggressive behaviors. These behaviors are usually vague or disguised as harmless comments, making it challenging to identify the underlying hostility.

As a result, you might feel emotionally drained, unsure of how to respond.

You could find yourself second-guessing your reactions, questioning whether you're being too sensitive or overreacting.

Subtle aggression can also make you feel isolated. As you deal with the constant undermining, you may withdraw, unsure how to explain what's happening.

It can be tough to talk about when others don't fully understand the situation or may even dismiss your feelings.

12. THEY CONSTANTLY BLAME YOU

Vulnerable narcissists are skilled at deflecting blame and avoiding any responsibility for their actions.

When confronted with their mistakes or shortcomings, they quickly point fingers at others, shifting the attention away from themselves.

Why

Vulnerable narcissists rely on blame as a shield to protect their fragile ego.

When they blame others, it helps them avoid the uncomfortable feeling of admitting their flaws. This allows them to maintain superiority and avoid taking responsibility for their mistakes.

It feeds into their belief that they're always right, entitled, and in control, even when they've clearly messed up. As a result, they come off as strong and unshakable, while the people around them are left feeling guilty or confused.

How

Vulnerable narcissists use various tactics to deflect blame.

One common approach is to shift attention away from their mistakes by pointing out your flaws. For example, if they forget something important, they might say, "You never help around the house," or "You're always so disorganized," making it about you instead.

They may also blame circumstances, other people, or their upbringing. For instance, they might say, "I only acted this way because of stress at work," or "I can't help it, it's how I was raised," avoiding any personal responsibility.

Another tactic is projection. They accuse you of the very behaviors they're guilty of. If they're being deceitful, they might call you a liar. This creates confusion and makes it harder for you to address their actions.

They might also drag others into the conflict to stay in control. They could tell a third party about your "complaints," making you seem unreasonable, forcing you to defend yourself in front of others.

If confronted, they may act confused. They might say, "I have no idea what you're talking about," or "I didn't realize I was doing anything wrong," even though they know exactly what they're doing.

The effect on you

Blaming keeps you stuck in a negative cycle. It prevents you from growing emotionally, resolving issues, or building healthier, more trusting relationships.

You might end up feeling guilty about things you didn't even do. This can make you feel inadequate, like you're somehow to blame for everything that goes wrong. You may start to doubt your worth, question your actions, or feel like you're always at fault, even when you're not responsible.

Blaming can also leave you feeling hurt, misunderstood, or unsupported. That can erode trust and intimacy in your relationships.

13. THEY ARE EMOTIONALLY UNAVAILABLE

Vulnerable narcissists are emotionally unavailable. They're so focused on their needs and insecurities that they struggle to tune into others or show empathy.

Trying to connect with them can feel like nurturing a plant that refuses to absorb the nutrients you're offering. No matter how much care, support, or understanding you give, it seems to have no effect.

In these situations, it's common to feel emotionally neglected or unseen. You may realize that you're giving more to the relationship than you're receiving.

Why

Vulnerable narcissists are emotionally unavailable because their world is shaped by fear, insecurity, and a need for self-protection.

They live in constant fear of rejection and criticism, making them hypersensitive to any perceived flaws or slights. This fear of being exposed prevents them from forming closer connections, as they worry about judgment and vulnerability.

To shield themselves from these fears, they keep interactions shallow and avoid emotional closeness.

They are also selfish and prone to anger. They expect others to meet their emotional needs, but rarely offer anything in return. When their expectations aren't met, they become frustrated and resentful.

This creates a one-sided dynamic, where their needs always come first, and others are left ignored or dismissed.

How

First, their emotional responses can be unpredictable. They switch from being very communicative to suddenly becoming silent, making it hard to understand their true feelings or intentions.

Their affection and attention also come with conditions, available only when it benefits them. When those conditions aren't met, they may withdraw or become distant.

Furthermore, they downplay your emotions to avoid dealing with them or validating how you feel. When you bring up their emotions or intrude on their personal space, they react defensively and push you away.

They could also intellectualize their feelings. They could talk about them in a detached way instead of expressing them directly, which creates a barrier to connection.

Additionally, they create excuses, drama, or crises to stay at the center of attention and avoid confronting emotions and needs.

When you seek emotional support from them, their response may be open or insincere.

Rather than offering genuine empathy or comfort, their reactions may seem more like a performance. Their focus tends to be on how they are perceived at the moment, rather than on authentically connecting with you or meeting your emotional needs.

The effect on you

Consistent emotional unavailability can leave you frustrated, unfulfilled, and neglected.

As a coping mechanism, you might start shutting down emotionally, pushing your feelings aside to protect yourself from more hurt. This detachment can make it tough to deal with your emotions healthily.

If you don't address these issues, you might end up repeating the same patterns of neglect and emotional distance in your other relationships, keeping the cycle of dysfunction going.

14. THEY GIVE CONDITIONAL LOVE, SUPPORT, OR VALIDATION

A vulnerable narcissist gives support in a way that keeps everyone around them unstable.

Their compliments and affirmations can come in waves. One moment, they're supportive, and the next, they are distant or indifferent.

But why does this happen? It's simple: their support is conditional.

Their validation shifts based on what they need at the moment, leaving you constantly on edge, unsure of what to expect.

Why

Vulnerable narcissists know that when you feel valued, you're more likely to be generous with your time, energy, and emotions.

That's why their "special" treatment is never unconditional. It's a strategy to create obligations and get something in return. They tend to offer support only when it serves their interests, and withdraw it once they've gotten what they wanted.

Furthermore, they give you just enough praise or validation to keep you hooked, but never enough to make you feel secure. This keeps you emotionally invested and constantly seeking more, while they stay in control.

How

Vulnerable narcissists carefully decide where to focus their attention based on their expectations, desires, or needs.

Then, if you meet their needs or align with their desires, they may offer you support, validation, or affection. However, if you fail to meet those expectations or challenge their control, their attention can quickly disappear.

Also, when you seek validation or support, they act busy and limit the conversation to their concerns or experiences. They briefly acknowledge your feelings but quickly shift the focus back to themselves, making their support insincere or shallow.

The effect on you

You might struggle to know where you stand with them. This makes it hard to set boundaries or make decisions. Their inconsistency can shake your emotional stability and leave you unbalanced.

Their conditional support puts pressure on you to act in specific ways to earn affection or approval. This forces you to constantly meet their shifting expectations, leading to emotional exhaustion.

Since their validation is tied to their needs, you may also begin to believe your worth depends on serving their interests. As a result, you'll waste more energy trying to maintain their approval than on taking care of yourself.

15. THEY MANUFACTURE LOVE TRIANGLES

Vulnerable narcissists use jealousy as a manipulation tactic to control others. To them, all victims are interchangeable, valued only for what they can provide.

To create this dynamic, narcissists manufacture love triangles. It's like their secret weapon. They will intentionally create or exaggerate rivalry between you and someone else, even if that other person isn't a threat. By doing this, they position themselves as the prize everyone is trying to win.

Why

The goal of love triangles is to provoke feelings of jealousy, insecurity, or desperation in you to create chaos that the narcissist can exploit to their advantage.

When you feel uncertain about your standing, you are more likely to seek reassurance, tolerate poor treatment, and compete for attention rather than question their actions. This feeds their ego, protects them, and reinforces their superiority.

It also directs power toward the narcissist. You may start complying with their wishes even when it goes against your needs or values. This self-adjustment reinforces their influence without them having to ask directly. The more reactive you become, the more control they get.

At the same time, love triangles allow them to switch between roles (victim, hero, or desired target) while carefully managing how they're perceived. This ensures that the narcissist remains at the heart of the drama, exactly where they love to be.

How

The vulnerable narcissists will subtly involve themselves with multiple individuals.

They begin with seemingly innocent interactions, using charm, emotional blackmail, and other manipulative tactics to cultivate close relationships with each person separately. Once these bonds are formed, they introduce the idea of others into the equation.

They use passive-aggressive tactics or indirect communication to sow seeds of doubt and jealousy. This may involve mentioning the other person in conversations, making comparisons, or affecting a lack of interest to heighten the perceived value of their attention.

When conflicts arise, the vulnerable narcissist quickly adopts roles such as the victim, the hero, or the wise one. This tactic turns the focus away from their manipulative actions and wins them sympathy and support from everyone involved.

In some cases, they may even escalate conflicts by exaggerating or making up stories to stir up more drama. This ensures the spotlight remains fixed on them.

The narcissist may also use a family member, such as their mom, dad, or siblings, to play a role in their love triangle games.

If you're in a relationship with a narcissist, there's a good chance they will create situations that make you feel like you're competing with their mom, dad, or other family members for their attention and approval.

The effect on you

You'll probably go through a cycle of negative emotions (jealousy, insecurity, and confusion).

The fear of rejection may loom over you, leaving you anxious and constantly seeking validation from them. You might question your worth and feel like you're falling short.

This experience can also shape your perception of love and relationships. You may come to view love as something tied to constant conflict, drama, and emotional highs and lows.

This can cloud your ability to recognize what healthy relationships truly look like. You might begin to accept unhealthy partnerships as normal, or even feel that love is only meaningful when it's intense and fraught with tension.

In the process, you may overlook or undervalue the qualities that define a genuinely healthy relationship. Things like trust, respect, mutual understanding, and open communication may seem less important compared to the chaos and validation you've been conditioned to seek.

16. THEY TRAIN YOU NOT TO ASK FOR ANYTHING

Narcissists are secretly competing with you for attention. They don't want you to steal their spotlight or outshine them in any way.

This constant competition forces your needs to take a backseat to theirs. They don't want you to have any needs because it threatens their control.

To stay in the spotlight, they train you to ignore or suppress your needs, ensuring that their desires remain the primary focus.

Why

Training you not to ask for anything makes them feel safe. It reassures them that their needs and desires will always come first, while your role is reduced to accommodating those demands.

When you don't ask for anything, they don't have to worry about meeting your needs or dealing with your concerns. It lets them avoid responsibility and keeps the relationship focused solely on their comfort and convenience.

How

When you need them the most, that's when they'll pull away or disappear. They'll come up with absurd excuses, like a sudden work crisis or someone else urgently requires them, leaving you stranded and alone.

When you also express a need, they might react with indifference or annoyance, subtly implying that your concerns are unimportant or unreasonable.

On top of that, they might respond with mockery or belittlement, making you feel like your needs are invalid.

They could also use guilt-tripping or shaming tactics to make you feel bad about asking for anything, suggesting that your requests are selfish. That makes you hesitate to speak up.

Finally, they may foster an environment where you become reliant on their approval and support. This dependency keeps you silent and focused on their validation, rather than on meeting your needs.

The effect on you

When a narcissist trains you not to ask for anything, it can severely damage your self-esteem. You learn to suppress your desires to keep the peace, gradually shifting into the role of a caretaker or people-pleaser focused solely on serving their needs.

This constant self-sacrifice leaves you drained and disconnected from your true self. Your self-importance fades away, making you feel invisible and powerless while the narcissist remains at the center, demanding more.

As your needs, wants, and boundaries become secondary, building new healthy relationships becomes difficult. You may struggle to assert yourself or advocate for what you deserve.

17. THEY CREATE DEPENDENCY

Narcissists create situations where you feel like you can't manage without them. They ensure you rely on them for emotional support, psychological clarity, and financial stability.

The goal is to make you dependent on them for your stability by positioning themselves as essential to every aspect of your life.

Why

Narcissists create dependency because it gives them control over your behavior and reactions to serve their needs.

For them, relationships are primarily a source of constant ego boosts. They thrive on your responses and use them to validate their self-worth. When they make you dependent, they ensure a steady flow of attention, which they crave.

Plus, your reliance on them empowers them to avoid taking responsibility for their flaws and toxic behaviors.

You might find yourself obligated to cover up their negative traits or make excuses for their behavior, making them more secure. They know your dependency means you're less likely to challenge or address their issues.

How

At first, they may help with your finances, manage your bills, or even make decisions about your daily life, like what car to drive or what groceries to buy. On the surface, it seems like they're just trying to take some burden off your shoulders. They'll claim they're only acting out of care, offering to handle these tasks to make your life easier.

But over time, they subtly tighten their grip. They use all the manipulative tactics we've discussed, making you increasingly dependent on them for decisions and everyday tasks.

It starts with love bombing. They mix their control with what feels like love, making you believe the more you depend on them, the stronger your bond becomes. Then, they make you feel like you owe them something for their "help," setting the stage for further manipulation.

They'll switch between idealizing and devaluing you. For example, if you try to make financial decisions without them, they'll criticize you or point out your mistakes. This reinforces the idea that you need their support.

They also gaslight and isolate you from friends and family, making it harder to turn to anyone else. They will make sure you have no access to money, a car, or a safe place to go.

Furthermore, they use emotional manipulation, conditional affection, blame-shifting, and projection to keep you emotionally dependent on them.

With unpredictable behavior, they ensure you're always seeking their approval. This keeps you stuck in a cycle of requiring their validation for emotional stability.

The effect on you

You may start to feel trapped, unable to make decisions or take action without their approval. You may automatically seek their permission for things that don't require it, like simple daily choices or financial decisions.

When they're not around, you might feel lost and anxious, doubting your ability to handle basic responsibilities without their guidance. This growing dependency erodes your confidence and leaves you feeling powerless.

If you try to escape their abuse, you may find yourself stripped of resources, power, and support. The narcissist's manipulation ensures that, when you attempt to leave, you're left with nothing.

This makes breaking free a complex battle. You will have to rebuild your life, regain your independence, and heal from the trauma they've caused.

18. THEY RUIN YOUR SPECIAL DAYS

For vulnerable narcissists, your special days are a stage for their drama and validation.

They thrive on being the center of attention, so events meant to celebrate you, like birthdays, anniversaries, or holidays, end up revolving around them.

If they don't get the attention they crave, they'll ruin your special day, creating drama, making you feel guilty, or turning it into a crisis. Their need for validation always comes before your happiness.

Why

Narcissists ruin your special days because they see your celebrations as a threat to their control in the relationship. Rather than supporting your happiness, they sabotage it to reclaim their sense of power.

Also, if your celebration brings you joy or highlights your achievements, it triggers intense jealousy. They cannot tolerate being in the background while you receive attention, praise, or recognition.

In their mind, any praise or acknowledgment you receive should be directed at them, as they believe they are the only ones deserving of admiration.

As a result, they turn your special day into a stage for their needs and emotions, ensuring that their dissatisfaction overshadows your moment.

How

First, they engage in attention-seeking behavior, like making self-centered comments or dominating conversations. They may interrupt others or talk over you to redirect the focus back to themselves.

They might also turn the special day into a chance to express feeling neglected or unappreciated. This shifts the focus from your celebration to their grievances, overshadowing your joy.

Sudden mood swings are another tactic. They may go from being cheerful to sulking, creating confusion and discomfort.

Narcissists also will try to convince you that the day isn't as special as you think. They'll criticize the way things are going or complain that things could have been "better" if they had been more involved. This undermines your joy and makes you question whether you even deserve to celebrate.

The effect on you

You might feel stressed, trying to manage the narcissist's moods and keep the celebration on track. This pressure makes it hard to enjoy the occasion or focus on your happiness.

You could also feel isolated because of their behavior. It creates tension, pushing away your guests or loved ones.

As a result, you might feel lonely during what should be a joyful celebration, with the narcissist's needs dominating everything.

Over time, this leads to resignation. Dealing with their drama makes you hesitate to plan anything special. You start downplaying or skipping celebrations to avoid the stress.

You also stop expecting to enjoy milestones and settle for a quieter, less joyful life, just to keep the peace.

19. THEY ISOLATE YOU FROM FRIENDS AND FAMILY

Narcissists don't like seeing you surrounded by people who support you, like family and friends.

They prefer to keep you isolated and dependent on them. This gives them more control over your emotions and decisions.

When you're alone, it's easier for them to manipulate you, with no outside influence or interruptions.

Why

Vulnerable narcissists isolate you to limit your options for advice, comfort, or assistance. They worry that these outside influences might weaken their control over you, making you less dependent on them for support and self-worth.

Besides, they're afraid that if you stay connected to a supportive network, their abusive actions could be exposed. Keeping you isolated helps them maintain their facade and avoid detection from others.

Isolation also ensures that they remain the sole focus of your attention and energy.

Finally, seeing you build positive relationships with others stirs their jealousy and insecurity. They resent the attention and care you get, feeling threatened that they're no longer the sole focus of your attention and energy.

How

They might subtly undermine your friends and family by criticizing or belittling them. This could involve making negative comments about their character, intentions, or behavior, which plants seeds of doubt and makes you question your connections.

During social gatherings, they may create conflicts or drama to make you feel embarrassed or uncomfortable. This behavior can push a wedge between you and your loved ones, making you less likely to invite them over in the future.

Vulnerable narcissists might also engage in smear campaigns to damage your reputation and credibility with your friends and family. They spread false rumors, lies, and negative narratives about you to alienate you from them.

On top of that, they may try to control your interactions with them. They might insist on being present during visits or phone calls, or come up with excuses to keep you from seeing people who support you.

The effect on you

Over time, your relationships with friends and family may start to suffer or even fall apart.

When you're cut off from loved ones, it's easy to feel isolated and trapped. This makes it harder to see the unhealthy aspects of the relationship. You also become more dependent on the narcissist.

Without external support, your mental health can worsen. The feeling of being stuck and alone deepens, making it even harder to find a way out.

20. THEY VIOLATE YOUR PRIVACY

Narcissists have a complete disregard for your personal boundaries. They routinely invade your privacy and attempt to control various aspects of your private life.

They might push past the limits you set or completely ignore them, leading to a cycle of ongoing disrespect and manipulation.

Why

Narcissists invade your privacy to gather information.

If they find something, they'll use it to their advantage, gossiping, spreading rumors, or even threatening you. All to protect themselves and feel more in control.

They also invade your privacy because they fear being left out or betrayed.

Sometimes, they project their insecurities onto you. If they're hiding something, they might assume you are too, leading them to snoop around to confirm or counteract their suspicions.

How

Narcissists invade your personal space without your consent. They may snoop through your private messages, emails, or belongings when you are not around.

In more extreme cases, they can become even more invasive, searching through your documents, rummaging through your room, or accessing your devices without permission.

Sometimes, they use manipulation or deceit to obtain private information, such as lying about their intentions or pretending to be someone else. For example, they might create fake social media accounts to trick you into sharing sensitive details.

Additionally, they may fake concern or interest in your personal affairs, subtly persuading you to reveal more than you intended.

The effect on you

When narcissists invade your privacy, they go beyond just accessing your personal information. They could also damage or destroy things that are valuable to you.

They might ruin documents, break special items, or tamper with your belongings, not just to cross boundaries but to undermine your security and assert control.

This behavior can leave you feeling deeply violated and frustrated, as it's not just about the loss of items but the breach of trust and personal space.

Also, if the narcissist shares or misuses the private information they've accessed, it can damage your reputation. This can affect your social standing, professional relationships, and overall self-esteem.

As a result, you might find yourself always on edge, being extra careful about whom you trust and what you share.

This constant alertness can make you overly suspicious of people's motives, even when they're completely innocent.

21. THEY ARE OBSESSED WITH PORN

Narcissists show an excessive and obsessive engagement with pornography, far surpassing casual use.

This intense fixation reveals their deeper psychological issues. It is a way to fulfill their cravings for control, validation, and dominance, all while avoiding genuine emotional connections.

Why

At its core, pornography objectifies people, reducing them to mere tools for sexual pleasure instead of recognizing their full humanity.

The individuals in these videos exist solely to satisfy someone else's desires, without any real emotional connection or concern for their well-being.

This kind of objectification aligns closely with narcissistic behavior. Narcissists crave control and gratification, and pornography provides a way to indulge these desires without the complexities of mutual respect and empathy.

Moreover, the lack of emotional connection in porn matches the lack of empathy that's common in narcissistic behavior.

This creates a cycle where their narcissistic traits are continually fed and reinforced, deepening their unhealthy attitudes toward sex and relationships.

The effect on you

Narcissists' obsession with pornography can damage physical and emotional intimacy in the relationship.

You might struggle to connect on a deeper level as they prioritize their gratification rather than building a shared emotional experience.

Pornography can also distort their view of sex and relationships, leading to unrealistic expectations and demands. They may pressure you to meet these impossible standards, which can be frustrating and damaging.

On top of that, they might constantly compare you to the people in porn to damage your self-esteem and make you feel like you're never good enough.

Finally, narcissists use their fixation on porn to manipulate the relationship. They may withhold affection or attention, keeping you off-balance and dependent on their approval. This is a tactic to maintain control and keep you under their thumb.

22. THEIR SEXUAL BEHAVIOR IS ROBOTIC, LAZY, AND AGGRESSIVE

Narcissists exhibit robotic, lazy, and aggressive behavior in bed, reflecting their broader personality traits. They put in minimal effort, focusing more on their convenience than creating a satisfying experience for both.

As a result, their actions become predictable, as they prioritize their pleasure over exploring your needs and desires.

Their behavior can also be aggressive, showing a need for dominance and control. They may push boundaries, pressure you, and prioritize their desires over consent and mutual comfort.

Why

Narcissists prioritize their pleasure over mutual satisfaction. They focus on their immediate gratification, rather than creating a shared, intimate experience. This makes the interaction feel shallow and emotionally unfulfilling.

Their regular exposure to porn can also desensitize them. They may require more extreme or novel stimuli to feel aroused or satisfied. This can lead to a robotic, detached performance in bed, and become less responsive to your cues.

The effect on you

The narcissist's lazy approach to sex can leave you feeling neglected and unvalued, impacting your body image.

Also, aggressive sexual behavior can cause trauma and anxiety. The hostility and pressure from aggressive actions create an unsafe environment, leading to fear and emotional pain.

These experiences can have lasting effects, potentially resulting in sexual dysfunction or aversion. This might manifest as difficulties with arousal or pleasure, or even a lack of desire to engage in sexual activity altogether.

HOW TO BEAT VULNERABLE NARCISSISTS?

INTRODUCTION

When dealing with a vulnerable narcissist, your first instinct might be to walk away.

For many, that's definitely the best course of action.

But sometimes leaving isn't an option; maybe you're emotionally invested, financially dependent, or tied together by family connections.

So, if you're stuck in a situation you can't just walk away from, what's your game plan?

The key is to learn how to manage the narcissist while still protecting your well-being.

In the next section, I'll share some practical strategies to help you navigate these tricky interactions and keep your well-being intact.

1. MANAGE YOUR EXPECTATIONS

You must accept this:

You are in a relationship with someone who has a personality disorder that prevents them from being capable of empathy, reciprocity, and genuine emotional intimacy. You cannot love them enough, be perfect enough, or sacrifice enough to heal their trauma.

They would need years of specialized therapy and, most importantly, a serious desire to change, which is rare. You will never get a sincere apology or acknowledgment of their inappropriate behaviors. They are incapable of seeing themselves as the "bad guy."

Therefore, "managing expectations" means you must radically adjust your understanding of reality to stop the cycle of disappointment and pain.

Learn to translate their behavior through the lens of their disorder. Expect nothing from them in terms of emotional support, consistency, fairness, or empathy. They are not a mirror of your feelings. They are a person with a disorder.

Once you learn this, you stop overexplaining, stop overgiving, and start noticing who responds to your presence rather than just consumes it. And perhaps most importantly, it also empowers you to leave early.

2. STAY COOL

Vulnerable narcissists are experts at fishing for your reaction. They thrive on stirring up emotions to get the validation or attention they crave.

So, if you stay cool and don't give them the reaction they seek, you can avoid falling into their trap.

When we say "stay cool," we're talking about how you present yourself (your vibe, demeanor, and attitude).

So, instead of jumping in with a knee-jerk reaction, take a moment and consider your response.

In your head, ask yourself: *"What is their goal right now? To provoke, to get sympathy, to start an argument?"* Then ask: *"What is my goal? To stay calm, to end the conversation, to maintain my boundary?"*

This 3-second pause transforms you from a reactor into a strategic responder.

If they make hurtful comments or engage in manipulative

behavior, respond with neutral, non-emotional answers. For example, when they disguise subtle insults as compliments, don't get pulled into their negativity. Stay calm and deflect it:

- **Them**: "You're surprisingly good at this for someone with your experience."

- **You**: "I appreciate the feedback." (Then, change the subject or return to the task at hand.)

This keeps the conversation from escalating and lets you turn their comment into something positive.

It's also important to keep your feelings hidden. While it's normal to feel upset when someone is trying to belittle or manipulate you, showing hurt or anger can give them more power to use against you. So, process those emotions privately.

Furthermore, when you're interacting with a vulnerable narcissist, your tone, and body language also play a huge role.

Keep your posture open and neutral, and avoid showing frustration, sadness, or anger in your expressions. The more composed you are, the less likely they are to push your buttons.

Remind yourself that their actions reflect their issues, not yours. This makes it easier not to take their behavior personally.

By doing this, you can stay grounded, avoid getting defensive, and respond thoughtfully instead of emotionally.

3. BE COLD AS ICE

Being "cold as ice" with a narcissist means maintaining emotional detachment and composure. It involves giving brief responses and avoiding the attention they seek, preventing their manipulative tactics from affecting you.

So, when they try to provoke you or stir up drama, stick to short, neutral replies. For example, if they say, "You never listen to me!" you can respond with, "I hear you," and leave it at that.

If they make dramatic claims or exaggerate, keep it matter-of-fact. Instead of getting caught up in their emotional turmoil, you might say, "I understand your point," and move on.

Also, when they seek excessive praise, keep your acknowledgment simple. Instead of showering them with compliments, a simple "Good job" or a nod can suffice.

If they share personal or emotional stories, listen politely but don't dive into emotional support. Try responding with something neutral like, "That's an interesting perspective," instead of getting drawn into a deeper conversation.

Furthermore, avoid sharing personal information. The less they know about you, the less they can manipulate or provoke you. Stick to objective facts rather than personal opinions or feelings.

If they ask intrusive questions, give vague answers or redirect. For instance, if they inquire about your plans, you could say, "I'm still figuring things out."

Avoid getting into arguments or lengthy discussions. If the conversation turns uncomfortable or manipulative, it's okay to end it or walk away. You might say, "I'd rather not discuss this topic," and move on.

If they try to draw you into personal conflicts, gently steer the conversation to a neutral topic. For example, if they start venting about their grievances, you can say, "Let's focus on finding a solution."

Also, adopt an attitude of indifference towards your reputation. For example, if they say something like, "Everyone thinks you're difficult to deal with," instead of defending yourself, you could respond with a calm, "That's interesting. I'm more focused on what I think and how I feel."

This shows you're not invested in their opinion, helping you rise above their drama.

Finally, resist the urge to seek their approval. Make your decisions based on your judgment and stick to them, rather than looking for their validation.

4. TURN THE TABLES AGAINST THEM

Turning the tables means taking the narcissists' manipulative behaviors and redirecting them back to them.

It helps you regain control and highlights the inconsistencies in their logic. Plus, it can distract them and shift the power dynamics, making them rethink their approach.

For instance, if a vulnerable narcissist tries to guilt-trip you by saying, "You never appreciate what I do," you could respond with, "I feel unappreciated too when my efforts go unnoticed." This might make them pause and reflect on their behavior.

When they seek validation, offer just enough acknowledgment while subtly pointing out their inconsistencies.

If they say, "No one ever appreciates my hard work," you could reply, "I understand that feeling, but there have been times when people recognized your efforts, like that big project you completed." This acknowledges their feelings while reminding them of past appreciation.

If they try to blame you, calmly ask them to explain their reasoning. For example, if they say, "I can't believe you didn't think of me," you could respond with, "I wish I could always think of everyone, but I have my needs too." This reinforces your perspective without escalating the situation.

And when they push your limits, assert your boundaries. If they say, "You should do this for me," you can respond with, "I can't commit to that right now." This reinforces your independence and takes away your control.

5. INSIST

When you start to gain the upper hand against a narcissist, they resort to familiar tactics to regain control. You might see gaslighting, shaming, love bombing, or blaming. They don't always get too creative with their strategies.

In these situations, you must be consistent in how you handle your interactions. If you stay detached and neutral, it becomes much harder for them to provoke or manipulate you. For instance, if they try to stir up drama, keep your responses calm and stick to your boundaries.

This approach helps you maintain your self-respect and assert your needs, even in a tough dynamic. If they start gaslighting or twisting your words, standing firm in your truth can help keep the conversation grounded.

And if they try to dominate the discussion or belittle your opinions, insisting on your perspective reinforces your autonomy.

Use "I" statements to frame your feelings, like saying, "I

feel uncomfortable when..." instead of "You always make me uncomfortable." This way, you reduce defensiveness on their part.

Also, be clear about what's acceptable and what isn't. If they cross a line, restate your boundary firmly and without apology. For example, you could say, "I won't engage in this conversation if you continue to raise your voice."

6. TREAT THEM LIKE A THIRD-PARTY

Seeing a narcissist as a third party, especially a family member, can create emotional distance. This perspective also allows for more objective interactions and reduces the emotional impact of direct engagement.

So, instead of viewing your narcissistic mother as a family member who controls your emotions, think of her as just another person in your life. This redirect can help you detach emotionally and better manage her behavior.

To treat the narcissist as a third party, consider using the strategies we discussed earlier, including:

- Manage your expectations

- Use neutral language

- Limit personal sharing

- Set clear boundaries

- Engage less emotionally

- Limit interaction

These are effective in maintaining distance and protecting your emotional well-being.

7. DOCUMENT INTERACTIONS

Documenting interactions with the vulnerable narcissist provides a clear account of abuse, helps process trauma, and can strengthen legal action or a restraining order.

Plus, it helps you separate your perceptions from actual events, especially in situations involving gaslighting or manipulation.

So, keep a dedicated note-taking tool for these interactions. Make sure to include the date, time, and any specific quotes if you can. This will give you a solid record to refer back to later.

Whenever you have a disagreement or notice any manipulative behavior, jot it down right away. Capturing your thoughts and feelings at the moment helps you stay accurate.

Don't forget to note when you set boundaries and how they responded. This is super helpful if they try to push those limits again down the line.

If you see any escalating behaviors that could lead to physical abuse, document those too. And if you can, take photos or videos of any physical evidence or save relevant messages that showcase their behavior.

CONCLUSION

We've explored 22 signs of vulnerable narcissism and 7 powerful tactics to regain control, but remember, there's so much more to discover.

Narcissistic behavior is complex, and as you continue on this journey, you may discover even more strategies that resonate with you.

Above all, remember this:

- You are not the problem. They are just reflecting their issues.

- You're not responsible for fixing them, and you definitely shouldn't take their outbursts or manipulative behavior as your fault.

- Their criticism, anger, and emotional games stem from their flaws, not from anything lacking in you.

The moment you realize that, you can start letting go of the weight of their actions and take back your power.